Nancy Wadman,

1st Prize

The Salvation Army
Sunday School
1965 - '66 - 66

Egermeier's FAVORITE Bible Stories

Egermeier's FAVORITE Bible Stories

Stories by Elsie E. Egermeier
Story Adaptations by Dorothy Nicholson
Illustrated by Clive Uptton

Selected Stories for Young Children

WARNER PRESS   Anderson, Indiana

TO BEGIN THE BOOK

This book has been prepared in answer to many requests from parents and church workers for a Bible storybook containing the best-liked stories from the popular and comprehensive Egermeier's Bible Story Book. These are especially adapted for children just under the normal age who read the Bible Story Book itself. The stories were selected on the basis of a survey of the favorites among children themselves and the observations of their parents. The size of type and the vocabulary is designed for the use of the younger reader. It is hoped that the stories will help open the Bible to these children as their interest in the stories presented here leads them to explore the Scripture references provided. The stories are also designed to be read to children not yet ready to read for themselves.

—The Publishers

Copyright ©, 1965, by Warner Press, Inc. Stories based on Egermeier's Bible Story Book, Revised Edition, Copyright, 1963 and 1955, by Warner Press, Inc. All rights reserved.
Printed in the United States of America
Library of Congress Catalog Card No. 65-11354

Thirty Favorite Bible Stories

Story	Page
1. The First People	9
2. The Great Flood	12
3. Abraham and Lot	17
4. Joseph and His Brothers	20
5. A Baby and a Basket	25
6. Crossing the Red Sea	29
7. God Gives the Ten Commandments	33
8. The Story of Ruth	36
9. The Boy Samuel	40
10. David and Jonathan	45
11. The Lame Prince	49
12. A Room for Elisha	52
13. Joash, the Boy King	57
14. A Little Girl Helps Naaman	61
15. Daniel in the Lions' Den	64
16. The Birth of Jesus	68
17. The Wise Men Follow a Star	73
18. When Jesus Was a Boy	77
19. Fishermen Leave Their Nets	81
20. Four Men Tear Up a Roof	84
21. A Boy's Lunch Basket	88
22. Jesus and the Children	93
23. The Good Samaritan	96
24. Zacchaeus Climbs a Tree	100
25. Jesus Rides into Jerusalem	104
26. The Last Supper	108
27. Jesus Dies on a Cross	112
28. Jesus Rises from the Dead	117
29. Paul Is Shipwrecked	120
30. The Philippian Jailer	124

The First People

Genesis 1:1—4:2

Long ago there was no world at all. But even then there was God, for he has always been the same God.

Then God made the world. He made day and night. God made the sky, the land, and the big seas. Next came grass and flowers, trees and plants on the land. After this God made the stars and the moon.

Then God began to make living things. He made all kinds of fish in the sea, and

Adam and Eve built an altar and worshiped God

all kinds of birds to fly in the sky. Then came animals in the woods and fields.

God knew that his work was good. But God had not ended his work yet. He planned to have people who would enjoy the earth and take care of it. They would know who had made all these things. More than that, they would be able to love and worship him.

So God made Adam, the first man. Later when Adam needed a helper, God made a wife for him. Her name was Eve.

Adam and Eve lived happily in their garden home. They enjoyed the good things God had given them. They knew nothing at all about evil or wrong.

But one day the serpent got Eve to eat some fruit from the one tree which God had said they must not touch. Then she gave some of the fruit to Adam and he ate it. They knew at once that they had done what God had told them not to do.

Because Adam and Eve did wrong, they had to find another place to live, outside the Garden of Eden. Now Adam had to work hard to get food for Eve and himself. Eve, too, had pain and unhappiness. And now they could no longer walk and talk with God face to face.

But they still worshiped God. They made altars out of stones and put gifts on the altars.

Adam and Eve must have been lonely for there were no other people. But God planned that there would be more people. A baby boy was born to Adam and Eve. They named him Cain. Their second boy was Abel. How they loved them!

Adam and Eve taught their boys about the great God, for they wanted their sons to love and please God.

The Great Flood

Genesis 6:11—9:17

Most of the people in the world were sinful and evil. But there was one man who tried to do right, and he taught his sons to do right also. His name was Noah.

Sometimes God talked to Noah. He told Noah that he planned to destroy the world because there was so much sin and evil. But he promised that Noah and his family would be saved.

"Build an ark," God told Noah. "When it is finished you and your family

God promised Noah that He will always care for man

will live there until the flood is all over."

Noah began building the great boat. God told him just how it should be made. How the people must have laughed at Noah and his sons! Here they were making a large boat, and no water nearby.

Again and again Noah told the people they should be sorry for their sins or they would be destroyed in the flood that was going to come. No one believed him.

When everything was ready, God told Noah to take his family into the ark. Then two of every kind of animal, bird, and creeping thing went into the ark. Seven pairs of each kind of useful birds and animals went into the ark. When all were inside, God shut the door.

Soon it began to rain. And such a rain! For forty days and nights it rained. Only

Noah and his family were safe as the ark floated on the waters.

When Noah sent out a dove and it came back, Noah knew the waters had not gone down yet. But when the bird brought back a leaf in her mouth, Noah knew the waters were drying up and the land was becoming green and beautiful.

God said to Noah, "Come out of the ark, with your family, and with all the animals." Noah went out the great door.

Noah was thankful to be alive. He made an altar and worshiped God.

God promised that he would never again send another flood that would destroy all living things. God said, "As long as the earth remains there will be springtime and autumn, cold and heat, summer and winter, and day and night." To remind men of his promise God made the rainbow in the sky.

Abraham and Lot
Genesis 13

Abraham was a man who worshiped God. He and his family kept sheep and cattle. They lived in tents near their animals. Sometimes they had to move so they could find grass for the animals.

One day God said to Abraham, "Leave this place. Go to a land where I will show you." Abraham trusted God, and so he took his wife, Sarah, and his nephew, Lot. With their workers and animals they went to a land called Canaan. God said, "This

"If you want the west, I will take the east"

is the land I will give to you and your children." Abraham built an altar and worshiped God. He and his family lived here in their tents for some time. The flocks and herds became larger and larger. Abraham grew rich.

When Lot, Abraham's nephew, was a grown man, he had many animals, too. Wherever Abraham and Lot went, it looked like a tent city. It took many tents for all the workers who helped care for the animals. The fields all around were dotted with sheep and cows.

Then Lot's workers and Abraham's workers quarreled. Each side wanted to take its animals to the best feeding places. Abraham saw how hard it must be for the workers. How could they always find places nearby where there was good grass and plenty of water? There was not room enough for all of them to live right there.

Abraham told Lot, "Let us not quarrel. There is not room enough for all of us to live here. But see, the whole land is before us. Let us separate. You choose which way you want to go. If you go east, I will take the land to the west. If you want the west, I will take the east."

God had promised to give all this land to Abraham. But he let Lot choose where he would like to live.

Lot thought, There is a river to the east. There will always be plenty of grass and water there. My flocks will get bigger, and soon I will be rich. Lot did not think about what would be good for anyone but himself. But Abraham let Lot take the land to the east.

Abraham trusted God and did as God asked. And as God promised, he blessed Abraham with many children and much land.

Joseph and His Brothers

Genesis 37; 39:1—46:7

Joseph was one of the great men in Egypt. Only the king had more power than he. But Joseph had not always lived in Egypt. As a boy he had lived in Canaan. His family were shepherds. Joseph had ten older brothers and one younger brother.

Joseph had been his father's favorite, and this made the others jealous. One day when father Jacob sent Joseph to see how the others were getting along, they were

How happy were Joseph and his brothers!

so angry with Joseph that they sold him to some men who were going to Egypt. They let their father think that Joseph had been killed by a wild animal.

In Egypt Joseph had many strange experiences. He was always a good worker, and God was with him.

One time the ruler of Egypt had a dream, and God helped Joseph know what it meant. Joseph said, "You saw seven fat cows, and that means there will be seven years when plenty of food will grow. Then you saw seven thin cows eat up the fat ones. After the good years there will be seven years when no food will grow. God has told you this so that you can store up food during the good years. Then there will be food to eat during the bad years." The ruler put Joseph in charge of storing the food.

During the bad years, Joseph's ten

older brothers came to Egypt to buy food. Joseph knew them at once, but they did not know him. Joseph said, "If you come again, you must bring your youngest brother with you."

When they needed food again, Jacob did not want Benjamin to go. But the older ones promised to take good care of him, and Jacob let Benjamin go with them.

Again Joseph gave them food. Then he decided it was time to let them know who he was. Imagine their surprise! But what a glad time for all of them.

Joseph sent wagons and men home with them, to help them move their families to Egypt to live. The old father, Jacob, could hardly believe the good news that Joseph was alive. How happy he was to make the trip to Egypt, along with the rest of his family!

A Baby and a Basket

Exodus 1:1—2:10

The ruler of Egypt had made the Israelite people slaves. He treated them very badly. At last the ruler said, "I must make life even harder for these people." So he made a new law that all the baby boys born to them must be killed.

It was about this time that Moses was born. How much his mother loved him! For three months she was able to hide the baby from the soldiers. By then he was getting too big to hide. What could she do?

They were surprised to see
a little baby inside

She gathered some tall grass that grew along the river and made it into a basket. To keep the water out, she put tar on the outside. Then she made a soft bed in the basket.

Next came the very hardest part. She put her baby inside the basket and carried the basket to the river. There among the tall grass at the edge of the water, she put down the little basket-boat and went home. Big sister, Miriam, played nearby and watched the baby.

Soon the princess came down to the river for a bath. She saw the basket-boat in the water. She sent one of her maids to get it and bring it to her. They all wondered what could be in the basket.

How surprised they were to see a little baby inside! He was crying. The princess knew at once that he was an Israelite baby whose mother was trying to protect him.

What could she do? "I'll adopt him as my own," she decided.

Miriam had been listening to all this. She ran to the princess and asked, "Would you like me to get a woman to take care of the baby for you?" The princess was happy to have an Israelite woman care for the baby.

Miriam ran home and brought her own mother quickly. How happy and thankful they were to carry the baby back home! No longer were they afraid of the soldiers, for everyone knew this baby had been adopted by the princess.

When Moses grew older, he was taken to live with the princess at the palace. Later Moses became a great leader of his people.

Crossing the Red Sea

Exodus 13:20—15:21

Moses led the people out of Egypt. God went with them and chose the way. In the day God was in a great cloud that moved slowly before the people. At night the cloud became fire, and God watched over them while they rested. Day or night, the people could look up and say, "Our God is going with us, and he is leading the way."

God led them to the Red Sea, where they camped beside the water. But all at

All the Israelites were safely across the Red Sea

once someone ran through the camp shouting, "Soldiers are coming!"

The people looked, and it was true. How frightened the people were! They could not swim across the Red Sea. They could not fight against the soldiers either.

Moses asked God for help. Then he asked the people to be quiet. "Do not be afraid," he said. "Stand still and see how the Lord will save you."

The cloud moved backward and stopped between their camp and the soldiers. To the Israelites the cloud became fire, and it lighted their camp all night. But to the soldiers the cloud was all darkness.

Then God told Moses, "Tell the people to go forward. Lift your rod over the Red Sea and divide it."

Moses did it, and God sent a strong wind. The wind made a wide path through the water and dried the ground. On each side the waters made a high wall. Every one of the Israelites and all their animals hurried toward the other side of the Sea.

When the cloud lifted, the soldiers saw the Israelites walking through the Sea on dry ground between two walls of water. They made it safely to the other side. The soldiers rushed after them. When they got far from shore, trouble began. Their horses got caught in the lines and their feet began to go down in the sand. The wheels began to come off their wagons.

"Let us go back!" the soldiers cried. But it was too late. The walls of water fell down, and they were all drowned.

At last the Israelites were free. They knew God had saved them. Moses wrote a beautiful song about the crossing of the Red Sea, and the people sang and rejoiced.

God Gives the Ten Commandments

Exodus 19—34

Moses was the leader of the people as they left Egypt where they had been slaves. God had shown Moses the way they should go.

Now they were camping close to a mountain. Moses went up the mountainside to talk with God. God told Moses the many laws he wanted the people to obey. Moses wrote God's words in a book.

When Moses came down the mountain, he told the people all that God had said.

Moses carried the two tablets of stone down the mountain

And the people answered, "All that God has said we will do."

Then the Lord said to Moses, "Come up to the top of the mountain and I will give you tablets of stone with the law and commandments written on them. Teach these to the people."

So Moses climbed the mountain again. For forty days Moses listened to God's words.

Moses was gone so long the people wondered if he would ever come back. They became restless. They soon forgot they had promised to obey the words of God.

One day they said to one of Moses' helpers, "We think Moses is not coming back. Make us gods to show us the way."

Now this man was not brave. He did not remind the people of their promise to serve no gods but the Lord.

The people brought gold. It was melted and made into the shape of a calf. Then the people worshiped the golden calf, as they had seen the people in Egypt do.

Just as the people were doing this, Moses came down from the mountain. In his arms he carried the two tablets of stone on which God had written the Ten Commandments.

Moses knew the people had forgotten the true God. He was very angry. As he came he threw down the two tablets of stone and they broke into pieces.

Later Moses asked God to forgive the people. And God wrote the Ten Commandments again on two other tablets of stone. This time the people were waiting when Moses came back from the mountain. This time they did not forget their promise to obey God's laws. They wanted to obey them.

The Story of Ruth
Ruth 1:19—4:22

The grain was ripe in the fields. Workers were busy cutting the grain and tying it into bundles. But they always left some on the ground for the poor.

Ruth said to Naomi, "Let me go to the fields and gather some of the grain that is left, so that we will have food to eat."

When Naomi had been a young woman, she had lived here in Judah with her husband and two little boys. Then they had

"Be kind to her, and be sure to leave some grain for her"

© 1965 Warner Press, Inc.

moved away. Now Naomi was an old woman, and Ruth was her young daughter-in-law. After Naomi's husband and her two grown sons died, she wanted to come back to Judah. Ruth had come with her to take care of her. Since they had no husband or father, Ruth had to find food for them.

It happened that Ruth went first to the field of a rich man named Boaz. When he came to see how his workers were getting along, he saw this strange young woman picking up grain. "Who is she?" he asked.

They said, "She is the young woman who has just come here with Naomi. She asked if she could pick up the grain that was left in the field. Ever since she has worked without resting."

Boaz watched Ruth as she worked. He knew she was trying to find food for

Naomi and herself. He had heard how good Ruth was to Naomi. No wonder he admired this pretty young woman.

Boaz told Ruth, "You may pick up grain after my workers every day. You may get a drink of water from my water jars."

When mealtime came, Boaz asked Ruth to eat lunch with his workers. "Be kind to her, and be sure to leave some grain for her," he told his workers.

Ruth was thankful for Boaz' kindness. Naomi was surprised when Ruth brought home a whole bushel of grain that evening. Ruth worked in Boaz' fields every day after that.

Later Boaz and Ruth were married. And they had a little boy named Obed. Naomi was glad to be grandmother to Obed. She helped Ruth care for him. How good God was to all of them!

The Boy Samuel

1 Samuel 1:1—2:21

Every year Hannah went with her husband to the tabernacle church to worship God and to take an offering. They loved the Lord.

But Hannah was unhappy because she did not have any children. More than anything else, she wanted a baby.

One year when Hannah went with her husband to take their offering, she told the Lord how much she wanted a baby. She prayed, "O Lord, if you will give me

"I have brought Samuel to help you"

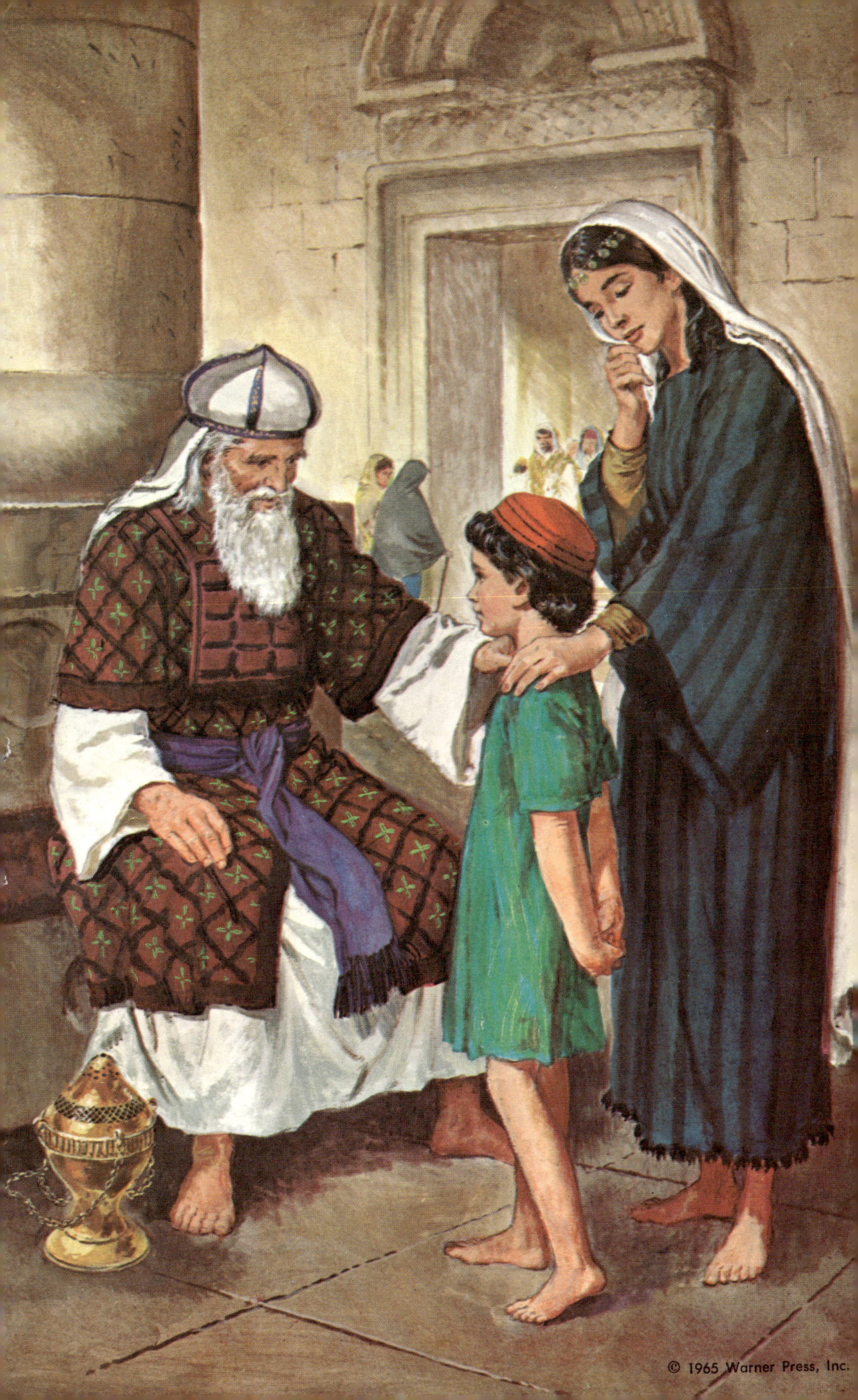

a baby boy, I will give him back to you to serve you all his life."

Eli, the priest, saw Hannah. He saw her lips move, but he heard no sound. He wondered what was wrong. Hannah said, "I have told the Lord all about it."

"Go in peace," Eli said, "and may God give you what you have asked."

Now Hannah was not sad. She knew the Lord had answered her prayer.

Before another year passed, God gave Hannah and her husband a baby boy. Hannah named him Samuel, which means "asked of God."

Hannah loved Samuel and took care of him while he was little. But after a while Samuel had grown big enough to be a real helper. Hannah knew it was time for him to go with them to the tabernacle church and to be a helper there.

She took Samuel to Eli and said, "One

year when I came here, I prayed for this child. Because the Lord answered my prayer, I have brought Samuel to help you in the tabernacle. As long as he lives he will belong to the Lord."

Eli knew God was pleased with Hannah. He promised to take care of Samuel and to teach him to serve God. Then Hannah and her husband went back home.

Every year after that Hannah went with her husband to the tabernacle church. She brought a new coat each year for Samuel. She was glad to see how much taller he had grown that year, and she was thankful when Eli told her how Samuel helped in the church.

Hannah was always glad that God had answered her prayer. And God gave Hannah other children besides Samuel.

© 1965 Warner Press

David and Jonathan
1 Samuel 20

When David was a shepherd boy, he played his harp for the king. Later David became an important leader in the army. The people began to think of him as a hero. They liked David better than they did the king. This made the king very jealous. At last he hated David so much that he wanted to kill him.

David was a very good friend of the king's son, Jonathan. David knew Jonathan would help him. He said to Jonathan,

Jonathan signals David by shooting an arrow

"Tomorrow is the beginning of the feast. The king will expect me to eat at his table. I will hide during the feast. If the king is angry because I do not come, you will know he means to kill me. But if he speaks well of me, then you will know it is safe for me to come back."

Jonathan promised to let David know. On the third day David was to hide behind a great rock in the field. Jonathan would come to shoot arrows. He would bring a little boy with him to pick up the arrows.

If he told the boy the arrows were on one side of the rock, David would know it was safe to go back home. If Jonathan told the boy the arrows were beyond him, David would know his life was in danger.

The king's family and guests sat around his table at the feast. David's place was empty. The first day the king said nothing about it. But when David was not there the second day, the king became very angry. Jonathan knew the king would try to hurt David.

The next morning Jonathan did as they had planned. When he and the boy were in the field, he put an arrow into his bow, and shot it. As the boy ran to pick it up, Jonathan shot another. Then he called, "The arrow is beyond you. Run, hurry, don't wait!"

The boy did not know this was a sign to David. After he got the arrows, Jonathan sent him back to the city.

David came out of hiding, and Jonathan ran to meet him. The two friends were sad as they said good-bye. Then David hurried away, and Jonathan walked back to the city.

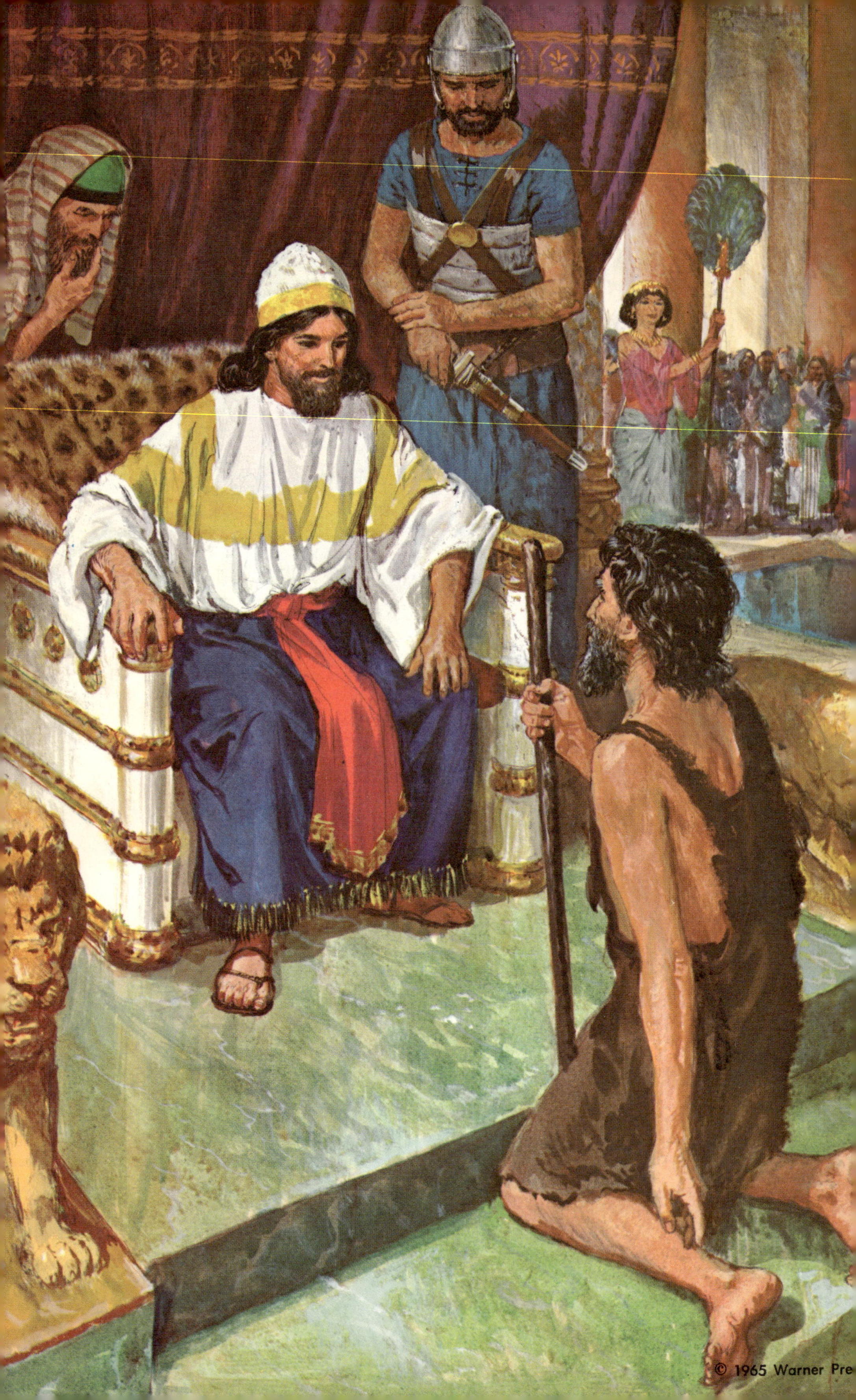

The Lame Prince

2 Samuel 4:4; 9:1-13

David was a great king. Sometimes he remembered that he had played his harp in King Saul's house when he was just a boy. David remembered, too, the good times he had had with the king's son, Jonathan. What good friends he and Jonathan had been! How much he had loved Jonathan!

But now both Saul and Jonathan had died. David wondered, "Where is the rest of the family?" When David asked, he was

"I knew your father well. He was my friend."

told there was one man who had worked for the family. He would know. David sent for him.

"Are any of Jonathan's family still living?" David asked. "I would like to show kindness to them."

The man said, "Jonathan has a crippled son named Mephibosheth. When he was a little boy, Mephibosheth had a bad fall. It made his feet crippled so that he could not run like other boys. Now he is a man and has a little boy of his own."

King David found out where Mephibosheth lived. He sent one of his men to tell Mephibosheth to come to the king's house.

Why would the king want to see me? thought Mephibosheth. He was a little bit afraid. But he went to see the king.

How glad David was to see Jonathan's son! He said, "Mephibosheth, do not be afraid of me. I want to show you kindness.

I knew your father well. He was my friend. I want to give you all the land that once belonged to your family."

Mephibosheth was surprised. He had not expected such kindness.

Then King David said, "I want you to come and live here in the king's house, too, and eat at my table every day."

King David sent for the man who had told him about Mephibosheth. "You will take care of all of Mephibosheth's farm lands," he said.

So Mephibosheth and his wife and little boy moved into the king's big house. Because Jonathan had been his friend, David was kind to Mephibosheth as long as he lived.

A Room for Elisha

2 Kings 4:8-17

Elisha went from one place to another, teaching people to love and serve the true God. He was called a prophet.

One day as he traveled he came to the little town of Shunem. Here a rich woman and her husband lived. They had many workers in their house, but they had no children.

When this woman saw Elisha and his helper, she invited them to come for dinner. She knew Elisha was God's prophet.

Elisha found that a room had been prepared just for him

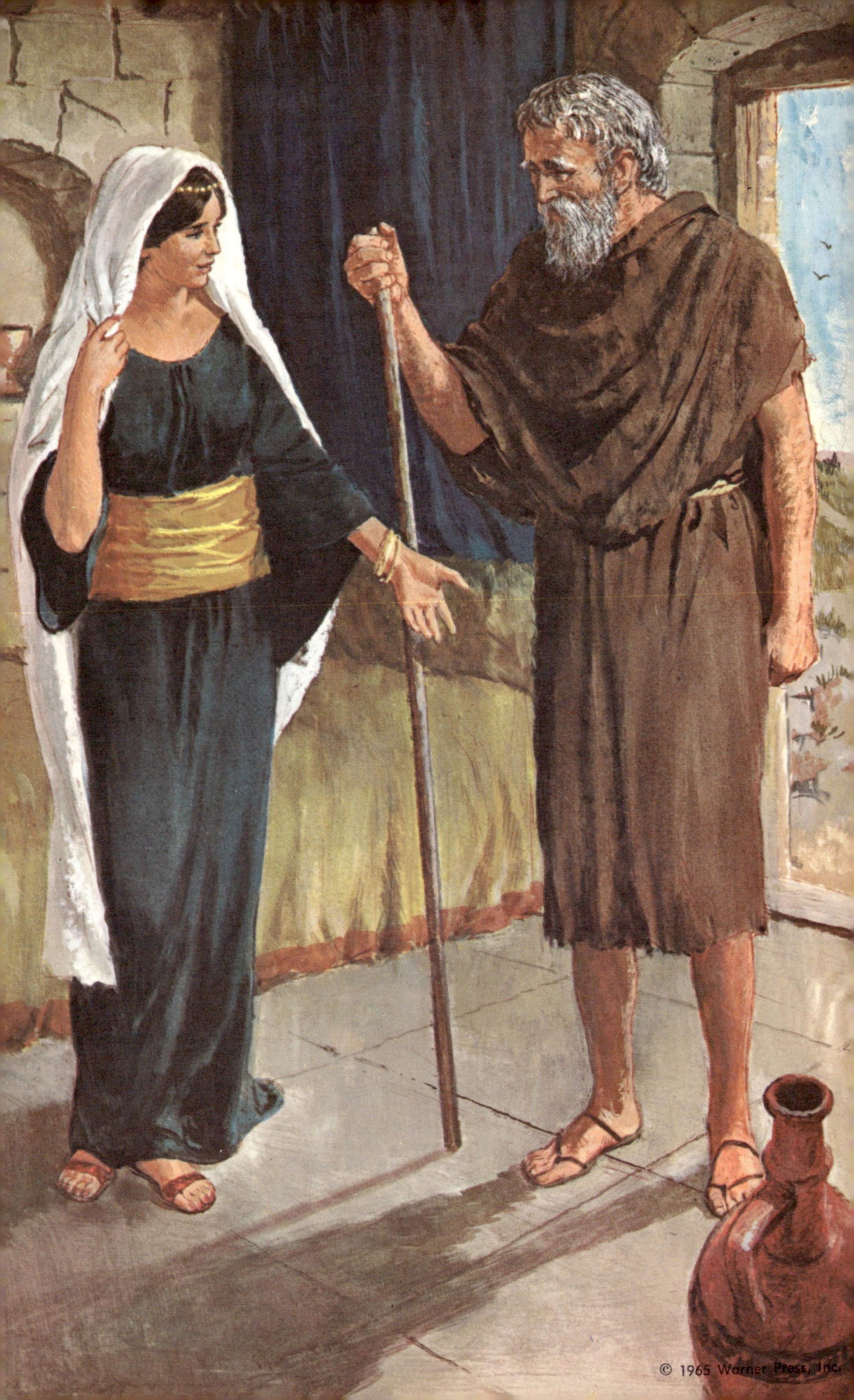

From that time on, Elisha stopped at her house when he came to Shunem. There Elisha and his helper could rest from their trip. And the woman fixed good food for them to eat.

One day after Elisha had been there, the woman had an idea. She talked to her husband about it. "Since Elisha comes through our town often, let's build a room on our house for him. We could put a table and chair in it, and a candlestick for light; we could put a bed in it. Then Elisha could stop here anytime, and he could rest whenever he wanted to."

The husband liked the idea. So they had a special room built for Elisha and his helper. They put into the room all the things Elisha would need to be comfortable.

Elisha did not know that these friends were fixing a room just for him. The next time Elisha came to Shunem, he had a happy surprise. The woman took him up on the flat roof of the house to the new room. She told him that it was for him, so that he could rest in a quiet place any time he wanted to when he was in their town.

How glad Elisha was for their kindness to him. "What can I do to thank you for this?" he asked.

The woman told Elisha she did not need anything. But Elisha found out that the woman and her husband wanted a child very much.

Before he left their house, Elisha told them that God would give them a son because they had been so kind to God's prophet. Time passed, and they did have a baby boy. What a happy family they were!

© 1965 Warner Press

Joash, the Boy King
2 Chronicles 22:11—24:3

Joash was only seven years old when he became king of Judah. He had never been allowed to run and play like other children. Always there was someone to watch and protect him. If his grandmother, the queen, had known about Joash, she would have had him killed. She was a wicked woman.

When Joash's parents died, his grandmother made herself queen. She did not know about the baby prince, Joash. His

When Joash was seven years old, he was made king

aunt and uncle had hidden him in a safe place for six years.

Many of the people did not like the queen. She was a heathen. Never did she go to worship in the beautiful Temple of the Lord. Instead, she worshiped in an idol temple. To make her temple prettier, she had her sons tear out the beautiful parts of the Temple of the Lord and put them in her place of heathen worship.

All this time Jehoiada, Joash's uncle, was busy planning a way to crown Joash king. When Joash was seven years old, his uncle called the leaders from all parts of the country to the Temple. He brought Joash to them and said, "Look at the king's son. He should be our king now."

The men agreed, but how could they make Joash king? Jehoiada said, "We will divide into three groups. One group will guard the doors of the Temple; another, the king's house; and a third, the gate. Here are swords and spears for those who guard the doors. They must not let the queen or her soldiers in."

Everyone did as Jehoiada said. Joash was brought out where all the people could see him. How glad the people were that he was alive and would become their king! How excited they were as they watched Jehoiada place the crown on his head! With a glad cry they shouted, "Long live the king!"

When the queen saw the crowds and heard the shouts of joy, she ran to the Temple. But Jehoiada ordered the guards to take her away, and Joash was the king. He was not old enough to rule the people by himself. Until he grew to be a man, his Uncle Jehoiada did that, Jehoiada taught Joash to love and serve God and to be a good ruler.

© 1965 Warner Press

A Little Girl Helps Naaman

2 Kings 5:1-14

In Naaman's house lived a young girl from Israel. She worked for Naaman's wife. Naaman was a brave captain in the army. But now Naaman had a sickness called leprosy. Naaman knew that the sickness would get worse and worse. Finally he would die.

The little girl was sad when she found out that Naaman had this sickness. How much she wanted to help Naaman and his wife! She told the wife, "If Naaman

The little girl told Naaman's wife that God's prophet could help him

would go to God's prophet in my country, the prophet would make him well."

People in Naaman's country had never heard about the true God, but Naaman's wife hurried to tell her husband what the little girl had said.

Naaman went at once to Israel. He waited outside while one of his men took a letter in to the king.

How upset the king of Israel was when he read the letter! "I am not God that I can make him well." The king did not know what to do.

But Elisha, God's prophet, sent a message to the king. "Send the man to me."

When Naaman went, Elisha sent his helper out to tell Naaman, "Go and wash in the Jordan River seven times. Then you will be well."

Naaman was angry. "Why should I wash in that muddy water when I can wash in clear water at home?" he asked.

Naaman's men knew that washing alone would never make Naaman well. They wanted him to do as Elisha said. If he did not, he might never be well again.

One said to Naaman, "If this prophet had told you to do something hard, would you have done it?" Naaman nodded his head. "Then why not do this little thing?"

Then Naaman knew this was right. He went to the river. He went down into the muddy water, one, two, three, four, five, six times, and nothing happened. But when he came out the seventh time, he was well.

How happy Naaman was! He went to Elisha and said, "Now I know there is no God in all the earth but yours."

Daniel in the Lions' Den

Daniel 6:1-23

Daniel was a fine young man. The king had learned that Daniel was good and wise. He knew he could trust Daniel. So when the king gave some helpers special work to do, he made Daniel the most important helper.

The other helpers were jealous of Daniel. They tried to catch him doing something wrong so they could tell the king. But they could not find anything wrong with Daniel. At last they thought of a way

"O Daniel, has your God saved you from the lions?"

© 1965 Warner Press, Inc.

to trick Daniel. Most of the people in this country did not worship God, but Daniel did. And these men knew how Daniel prayed each day to God.

The men said to the king, "We have a new law we want you to make. For thirty days no one can ask anything of any god or man, except you, O King. And if anyone does, he will be put into the lions' den." The king liked being the most important man in all the kingdom, and so he made the law.

Daniel heard about the law, but he did not obey it. Just as before, he prayed by his open window. The men who were jealous of him saw him there, thanking God.

They hurried to the king. "Daniel has not obeyed your law," they said. "Three times today he has prayed to his God."

How upset the king was! How sorry

he was that he had listened to these men and made such a law! All day he studied the laws of his country, trying to think of some way to save Daniel.

When the sun went down, the men came back, and the king knew he could not save Daniel. He had Daniel put into the lions' den. The king told Daniel how sorry he was to do this. "Your God will surely save you from the lions."

That night the king could not eat or sleep or listen to music. He kept thinking about Daniel. As soon as it was light, the king went to the lions' den. "O Daniel, has your God saved you from the lions?"

The king listened. From the deep pit he heard Daniel say, "God sent an angel to shut the lions' mouths. They did not hurt me. God knew I had done no wrong."

How glad the king was! He had Daniel taken out of the pit at once.

The Birth of Jesus
Luke 1:26—2:20

Everyone was excited about the new law. It said all must go to the town from which their families came. This was to be done so that all the people living in the country could be counted.

Mary and Joseph had to go to Bethlehem. It was a long way. Many other people were going too.

As they went Mary must have thought about the angel's visit to her. God had sent an angel to tell Mary that she would

The shepherds saw little Jesus lying in a manger

© 1965 Warner Press, Inc.

have a baby boy. The angel had said that the baby would grow to be a great man. He would be a king who would rule forever. The angel had told Joseph, too, and they had waited eagerly ever since for the baby to come.

When they got to Bethlehem, the city was crowded with people. They could find no room in which to stay. The trip had been hard. How much Mary wanted a place to rest! She knew that soon it would be time for her baby to be born. At last Joseph found a stable where it was warm and quiet. There was fresh hay to rest upon.

That night Mary's baby was born. She wrapped him in soft cloth and laid him in a manger.

Shepherds were watching their sheep that night near Bethlehem. Suddenly the angel of the Lord came near. A great light shone in the sky. The shepherds were afraid. Why had the angel come to them?

The angel said, "Do not be afraid. I bring you good news for all people. In Bethlehem today a Savior is born. He is Christ the Lord. You will find him lying in a manger."

What wonderful news! Many angels sang, "Glory to God in the highest! On earth peace, goodwill to men."

The shepherds said to one another, "Let us go now to Bethlehem. We must see this." So they left their sheep and hurried to Bethlehem. They found Mary and Joseph. They saw little Jesus lying in a manger. When the shepherds left, they were thanking God for all they had seen and heard. They told everyone they met about it.

Mary never forgot what happened that night, nor what the shepherds told her.

© 1965 Warner Press

The Wise Men Follow a Star

Matthew 2:1-15

Some Wise Men who lived in the East had seen a bright new star in the sky. By this God made them know that Christ had been born.

At once they planned to go to see this child. They would take rich gifts. They would worship him, for he was sent by God. It was a long trip. But they kept going, with the bright star as their guide.

When they came to the country where Jesus was born, they hurried to the king's house. "Where is the child who will be king of the Jews?" they asked. "We have seen his star in the East. We have come to worship him."

Herod was upset and worried. What can this mean? he thought. Herod knew nothing about a new king. So he asked his helpers about it. They read to him from the Scriptures that Bethlehem was the place where the Savior would be born.

Now Herod was more worried than before. Herod did not want another king around. If he could just find out where this new king was, he would get rid of him.

Herod said to the Wise Men, "Go to Bethlehem. Look for the child until you find him. Then come and tell me so that I can go and worship him, too."

As the Wise Men went toward Bethlehem, they saw the same bright star they had seen in the East. It seemed to lead them. Surely God was helping them find Jesus.

At Bethlehem the star stood still over the place where Jesus was. At last they had found the newborn king! They went into the stable and saw Mary and little Jesus. They knelt down and worshiped him. Then they gave him rich gifts—gold, frankincense, and myrrh.

God told the Wise Men in a dream not to go back to Herod. So they went home by another road.

Soon after this God told Joseph, "Get up! Take the young child and his mother. Hurry to Egypt. Stay until I tell you to come back. For Herod will try to find and kill Jesus." Quickly Joseph took Mary and Jesus to Egypt.

Herod was angry when the Wise Men did not come back. He looked for Jesus, but Jesus was safe in Egypt.

© 1965 Warner Press

When Jesus Was a Boy
Luke 2:40-52

As a little boy, Jesus loved to watch Joseph work. He played with the shavings that fell from Joseph's workbench. He liked to run and play outdoors with his friends, too. Each week they went to the synagogue in their town to worship God.

When Jesus was old enough to go to school, Mary and Joseph sent him to the synagogue in Nazareth. Here he learned to read and write. Like other Jewish boys, Jesus learned many Bible verses by heart.

Mary and Joseph found Jesus in the Temple

One spring morning a group of Jews left Nazareth to go to Jerusalem. At the temple they would go to special services called the Feast of the Passover. Mary and Joseph went every year, but this year they were taking Jesus with them for the first time. He was twelve years old.

As they traveled, people from other cities and towns joined them. At Jerusalem they met more people—people from every part of the land. What an exciting time this was! How wide Jesus' eyes must have been when he saw the Temple!

Each day at the Temple Jesus listened to the wise teachers. He asked many questions. Jesus began to understand that God was his Father, and that he must work with God.

At the end of a week it was time to go home. As they started out, Mary did not see Jesus. But she thought he was with some of the group. Evening came. Still Mary did not see Jesus. She and Joseph began to ask, "Have you seen Jesus?" But no one had seen him that day.

Now Mary and Joseph were very worried. They went back to Jerusalem, hunting for Jesus. They looked and looked. At last they found him. Jesus was at the Temple with the wise teachers, asking questions and listening.

Mary said, "Son, why did you stay here when we were starting for home? We have been very worried. We've looked everywhere for you."

"Didn't you know that I would be at my Father's house?" Jesus asked.

They all went home to Nazareth. As the years passed, Jesus grew to be a fine young man. He learned to explain the Scriptures and to talk with God. His kind, thoughtful ways won him many friends.

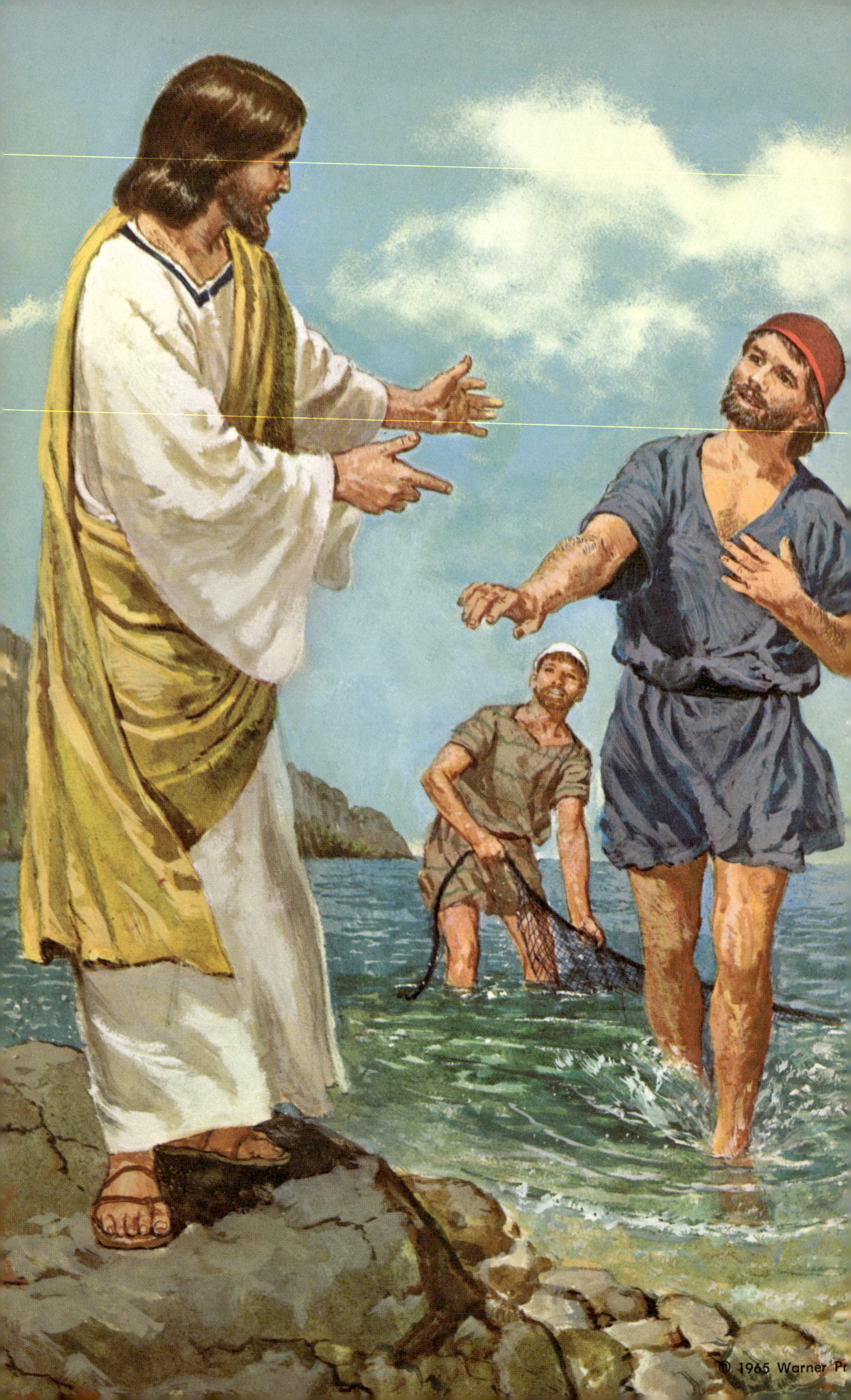

Fishermen Leave Their Nets

Mark 1:16-38; Matthew 4:18-23

One day Jesus was walking on the rocks by the water. He saw two men fishing. They were named Simon and Andrew. Jesus called to them, "Follow me." Simon and Andrew came right then to Jesus and went with him. They believed that Jesus was the one which God had promised to send. Being with Jesus was more important than catching fish.

As the three men walked along the shore they saw two other fishermen mend-

Jesus calls two fishermen to follow him

ing their nets. These brothers, James and John, worked with Simon and Andrew in fishing. Jesus called these two to follow him also. At once they left their boat to go with Jesus.

Taking the four fishermen, Jesus went back to the city. On the day for worship they all went to the church. There Jesus taught the people. When Jesus spoke they felt as if God were talking to them. A sick man was there, and Jesus made him well. How surprised the people were! Never before had they seen anyone do things like this.

Then Jesus and the four fishermen went to the house of Simon and Andrew. There they learned that Simon's mother-in-law was sick with a fever. They brought Jesus to her. Taking her hand, Jesus lifted her up and the fever left at once. She felt so well that she got up, and she helped get the meal for Jesus and the others.

Just at sunset many people began to come to Simon's house. Some carried sick people in their arms. Others led the blind. Some came helping friends who had a hard time walking. Everyone wanted Jesus to make their friends or loved ones well.

What a busy time it was! Jesus was glad to help the people. Many people were made well that night by Jesus.

The next day other people came looking for Jesus, wanting him to help them. But Jesus told his fishermen friends, "I must go on to other towns. I must teach people there also. This is the work I am to do for God." So the four new friends went with Jesus to many places, helping him with his work.

Four Men Tear Up a Roof

Mark 2:1-12; Luke 5:18-26

One day Jesus came back to the city where he was living. He had been away on a trip. Very soon people began to say to each other, "Jesus is home again." Before long, people began to come to see Jesus. More and more people came. Some came because they wanted to see their friends again. Others came to ask Jesus to help them. There were all kinds of people in the crowd.

They pushed into the small house until

Jesus told the sick man, "Get up from your cot"

© 1965 Warner Press, Inc.

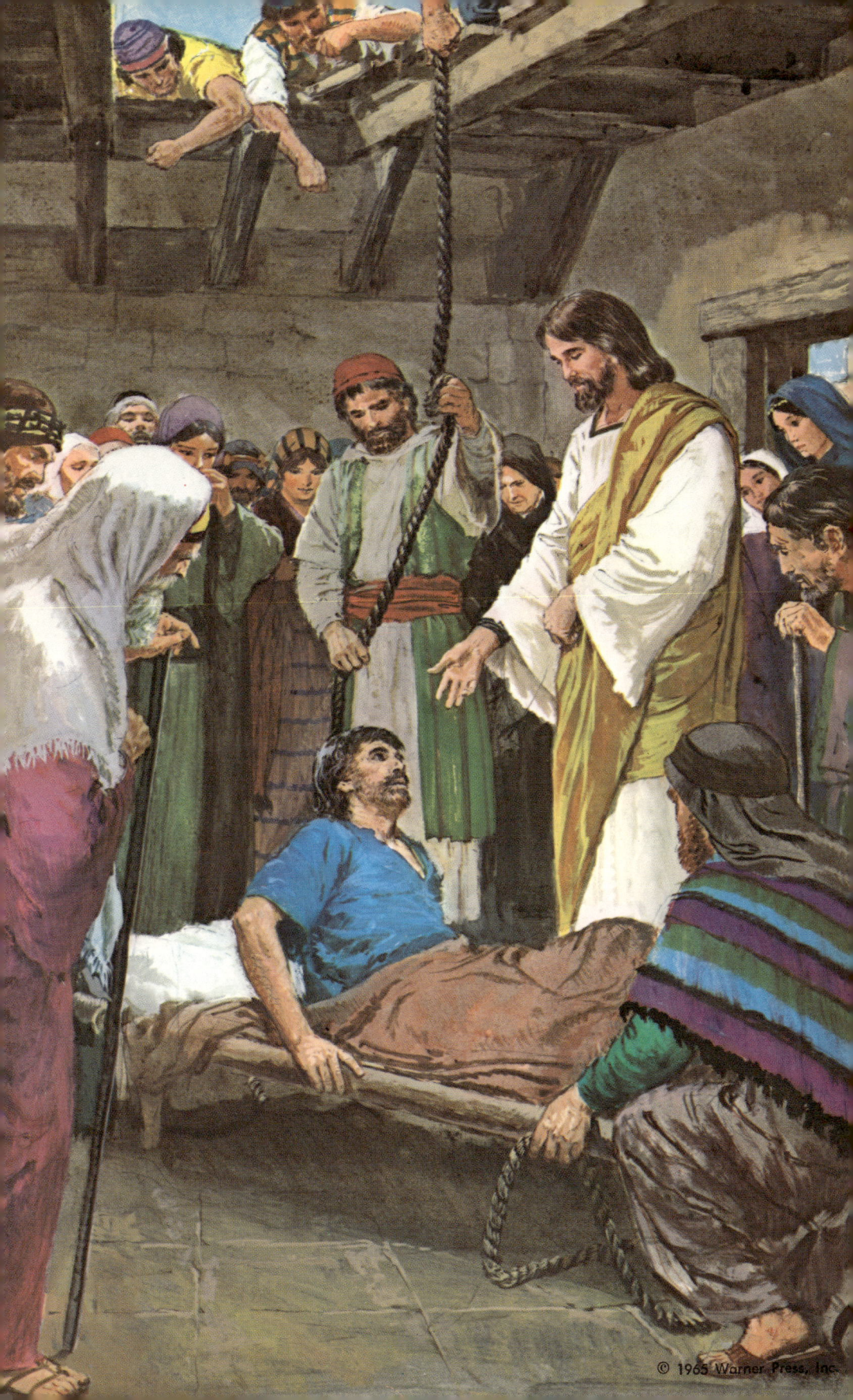

no more could get in. Others filled the doorway, trying to see and hear what was going on inside. Jesus made the sick ones well. He taught the people also.

As they listened to Jesus, they began to hear noises above them. Soon there was a hole in the roof. What was happening? The hole grew bigger and bigger. Then they could see men on the roof and a sick man on a cot.

When the hole was big enough, the men tied ropes onto the cot and let it down into the room, right in front of Jesus.

The sick man's four friends looked through the hole. Would Jesus make their friend well? He could not move about by himself. Day after day he had been in bed, sick and helpless. His friends had tried to bring him to Jesus. But they could not get through the door because of the crowd. So they had gone up to the roof.

The people in the room were very much surprised. They wondered what Jesus would do. Jesus knew that the four friends had wanted very much to bring the sick man to him. Jesus knew that the friends believed that he could make the sick man well.

And that is just what Jesus did. He told the sick man, "Get up from the bed. Fold up the cot, and go back to your own house now."

At once the stiffness left the sick man's body. He was strong again. He got up, rolled up the cot, and walked out. The people were so surprised that they made way for him to get through. The people knew that it was God who had done this. As they went home, they said, "We have never seen anything like this before!"

A Boy's Lunch Basket

Matthew 14:13-23; Mark 6:30-46

Jesus' helpers had just come back from a trip. They could hardly wait to talk to Jesus about it. But wherever Jesus was, people came to see him. He did not have time to rest or even to eat. So Jesus called his helpers and said, "Come with me to a quiet place where we can rest and talk."

They got into a little boat and sailed to the other side of the lake. No towns or people were there, and it was quiet. Surely they could be alone for a while.

"Here is a boy with five buns and two fish which he will share"

© 1965 Warner Press, Inc.

But when they came to the shore, they saw many people. Someone had seen Jesus and his helpers leave. They knew where they might go. The people had no boats, but they wanted very much to be with Jesus. So they hurried along the rocks at the edge of the water and were waiting when the boat got to the other side.

Perhaps the helpers were a little sorry that the people had found them again. But Jesus looked at the people lovingly.

Jesus got out of the boat. Sitting on the shore, he taught the people and made the sick ones well.

Evening came. Still the people stayed. They seemed to forget they could not find food or rooms for the night way out there. Jesus' helpers said, "Send them away so they can buy food as they go home."

But Jesus answered, "We must feed them before we send them home."

Philip looked at all the people and shook his head. "If we went to town and spent two hundred silver coins to buy bread, it would not be enough," he said.

When they had left home, the people had not known they would have to go so far to find Jesus. One boy, however, had not forgotten to bring his lunch basket. In it were five loaves of bread and two fish.

The boy heard them talking. He was willing to share his lunch if it would help. He took his lunch to Andrew. Andrew said to Jesus, "Here is a boy with five buns and two fish which he will share. But what will that be among so many people?"

Jesus said, "Have the people sit down." Then Jesus gave thanks and broke the food into small pieces. His helpers passed it around, and all those hungry people had enough to eat.

© 1965 Warner Press

Jesus and the Children

Mark 10:13-16; Luke 8:41-42, 49-56;
John 4:46-53

Everywhere Jesus went, many people followed him, asking him to help them and listening to the things he taught. One day while Jesus was teaching the people, mothers brought their little children. They wanted Jesus to put his hands on the children and pray for them.

When Jesus' helpers saw the mothers and children, they did not like it. They thought Jesus was too busy to talk to boys and girls. They said, "You can see how

Jesus was happy to have the children come to see him

busy Jesus is. Go away. He cannot talk to children now."

Jesus heard what his helpers said. He saw the mothers and children. He could see how sad they were. Jesus said, "Let the children come to me. Do not try to stop them." And Jesus took the little ones in his arms. He was happy to have the children come to see him.

On another day a father came running to Jesus. "My little girl is very sick. But if you will come and put your hands on her, she will get well," he said.

At once Jesus started to go with the father. Before they got to the house, a man came with sad news. "Your little girl is dead," he said. "It is no use to bring Jesus now."

But Jesus said, "Do not be afraid. She will be made well." And they went on to the house. Jesus, with the mother and father, went into the girl's room. He took the girl's hand, and said, "Little girl, get up!" She opened her eyes, got up, and walked about the room, well again.

Another time Jesus helped a sick boy. His father asked Jesus to go to the boy and make him well. Jesus told the father, "Go back home. Your boy is well."

The father started home. On the way a servant came running. "The boy is well!" he shouted.

"At what time did he begin to get well?"

When the servant said, "Yesterday at seven o'clock," the father knew that this was the same time Jesus had said, "Go home. Your boy is well." Jesus had made him well.

The Good Samaritan

Luke 10:25-37

One day a man said to Jesus, "The Bible says to love God with all your heart, soul, mind, and strength. It says to love your neighbor as yourself. But who is my neighbor?"

To answer him Jesus told this story:

"One day a man took a trip. He walked along the lonely road from Jerusalem to Jericho. On the way some robbers stopped him. They took away his money. They tore off his clothes and beat him.

The Good Samaritan took care of the sick man

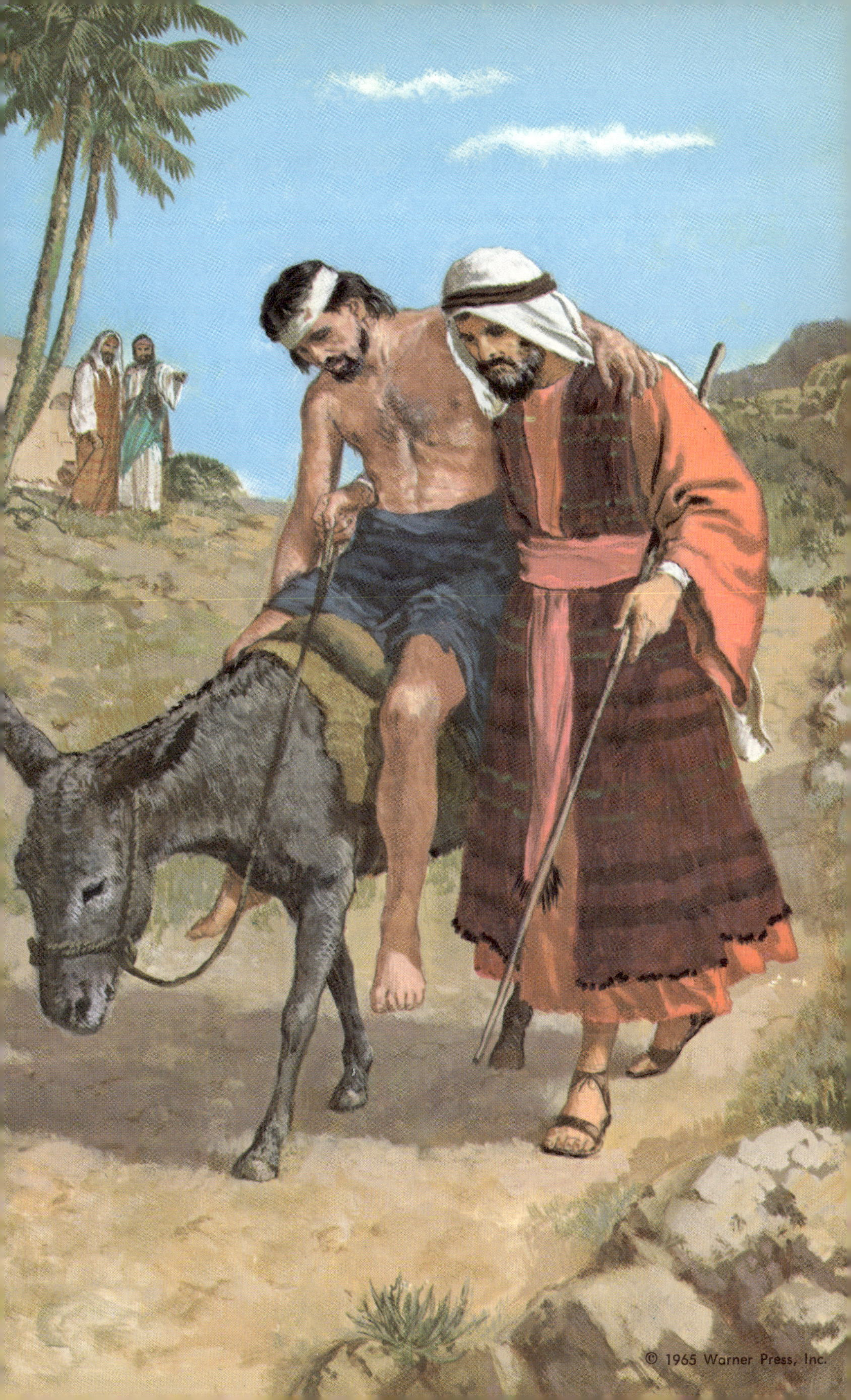

Then they left him badly hurt beside the road.

"After a while a priest came down the road. He saw the man who had been hurt. But he did not stop to help him. He did not even say a kind word to the poor man.

"Next a priest's helper came along. He saw the hurt man lying there by the road too. But he just looked and hurried on. He did not even try to help the man.

"Perhaps the man would have died if a kind person had not come along. A man riding on a donkey came along this same road. He was called a Samaritan because he lived in a country called Samaria. The Samaritan rode up to where the hurt man lay. He saw that the man needed help. At once he stopped his animal and climbed down to help. The hurt man was a Jew. And Jews were not friends with Samaritans. But the kind Samaritan felt he must help this Jew who was in great trouble.

"First he poured medicine on the hurt places. Then he bandaged them. After that, he lifted the man up onto the animal and took him to a hotel in the next town. There he took care of the sick man.

"On the next day the Samaritan had to go on his trip. So he went to the hotel man and gave him some money. Then he said, 'Take care of this man until he is well. If you need more money than this, I will pay it when I come back this way.'"

Jesus looked around and asked the man, "Now which of these three men was a neighbor to the one who was hurt by robbers?"

The man answered, "The man who was kind to him."

And Jesus said, "You go and do the same."

Zaccheus Climbs a Tree

Luke 19:1-10

A rich man named Zacchaeus lived in Jericho. The people had to pay many taxes. Zacchaeus was one who collected the tax money. In fact, Zacchaeus was the one who was over all the other tax collectors. He was the chief. The people did not like Zacchaeus. They said he took more money than he should when they paid taxes. They said Zacchaeus was not honest.

One day Zacchaeus heard that Jesus

How surprised Zacchaeus was! Jesus wanted to go home with him.

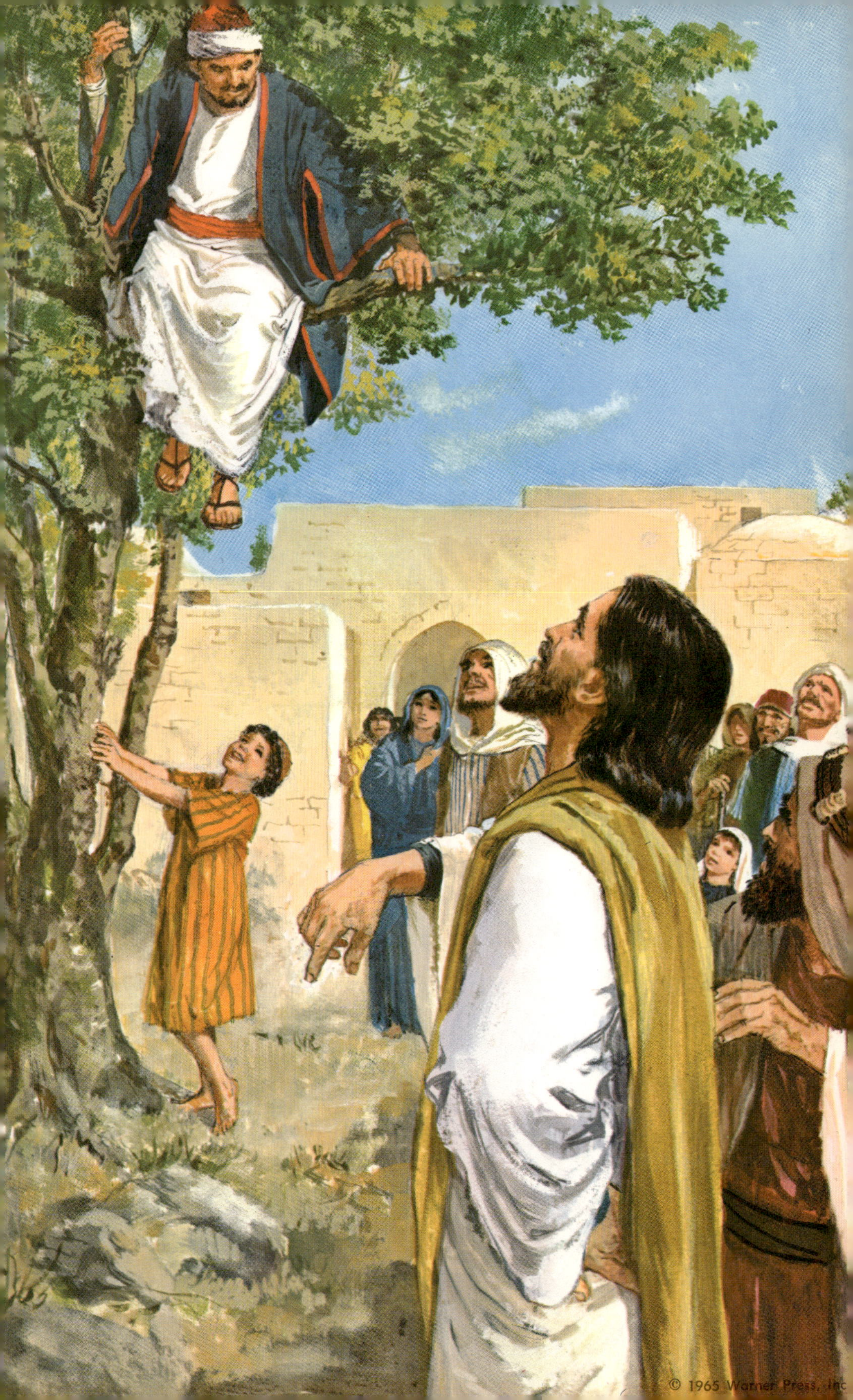

was coming through Jericho on his way to another city. Zacchaeus wanted more than anything else to see Jesus.

Many people stood along the road where Jesus would pass by, waiting to see Jesus. Zacchaeus stood with them at the side of the road. But he could see nothing. He was too short to see over the heads of the others. What could he do?

He ran down the road to a large tree. He climbed up that sycamore tree and sat on a branch. Now he was up above the others. Surely he could see Jesus from this place.

Jesus and the men with him came along the road. All the people tried to see Jesus. On they walked until they came to the tree where Zacchaeus was. Here Jesus and his friends stood still. Jesus looked up into the tree. He saw Zacchaeus sitting there.

"Zacchaeus," called Jesus, "come down at once, for today I must stop at your house."

How surprised Zacchaeus was! Jesus wanted to go to his house for dinner! He could take Jesus home with him.

Zacchaeus was happy as he led the way to his house. As they went, others followed them. Some thought it was wrong for Jesus to go to the house of a tax collector. "Zacchaeus is not a good man," they said.

Zacchaeus and Jesus talked. Zacchaeus was changed by Jesus' kind words. He told Jesus, "I will give half of all I have to the poor. And if I have taken more from any man than I should, I will give back four times as much as I took."

Jesus was glad to hear Zacchaeus say that. Jesus knew he had helped Zacchaeus, and this was why Jesus had come.

Jesus Rides into Jerusalem

Matthew 21:1-11; John 12:12-19

All Jerusalem was excited. Many people had come to the city for the special services called the Feast of the Passover.

Jesus knew that in Jerusalem were some very important men who did not like him. Somehow he knew that these men would try to kill him. But Jesus planned to go to Jerusalem anyhow for the Passover. This was what his Father, God, wanted him to do.

When Jesus and his helpers (or di-

The crowds cheered as Jesus rode into Jerusalem

© 1965 Warner Press, Inc.

sciples) were getting near to the city, the people in Jerusalem heard that they were coming. Crowds of people hurried out through the city gate to a hill outside the city. They wanted to meet Jesus because they had heard so much about him.

As Jesus and his disciples were walking toward Jerusalem, they stopped. Jesus said to two of them, "Go to the town near here. As you go into town you will see a colt that has never been ridden. Untie him and bring him to me. If anyone asks, 'Why do you do this?' say, 'The Lord needs him and will send him back right away.' "

The two disciples went to the town, found the colt and untied it. Some asked, "Why are you doing that?" But when they heard that Jesus needed the colt, they let it go.

The disciples brought the colt to Jesus. They put their coats on its back. Then

Jesus sat on the colt and rode down the hill to the city.

Many people put their coats on the ground. Others put green branches down. It was like a bright rug for Jesus to ride over. Some people waved branches in the air. They sang and shouted. They were happy and gay, singing praise to God and to Jesus.

Such a parade they made, coming into the city! Such a noise their singing and shouting made! Such a crowd of people all around Jesus as he rode on the little colt! Other people hurried into the street to see what was happening. "Who is this?" they asked.

The crowd answered, "This is Jesus, the teacher from Nazareth."

The Last Supper

Matthew 26:17-30; Mark 14:12-26;
Luke 22:7-39; John 13

Jesus asked Peter and John to fix the special supper for the Passover.

"Where shall we go to fix this meal?" they asked Jesus.

"Go into the city. There you will meet a man carrying a pitcher of water; follow him. When he gets to his house, say to him, 'Where is the guest room where Jesus is to eat the Passover with his disciples?'"

The two went their way. It was as Jesus had said. The man of the house took them

Jesus and his disciples eat their last meal together

© 1965 Warner Press, Inc.

to a room upstairs. Probably he knew Jesus and was glad to have him use the room.

Peter and John fixed everything for the supper in just the right way. When evening came Jesus and the other ten disciples joined Peter and John. They all sat down at the table and ate the supper.

They felt very sad when Jesus told them that this was his last supper with them. Would Jesus really be taken away from them? It seemed impossible to think that men ever could kill him.

Soon they were talking about other things. Some wondered who would be greatest in Jesus' kingdom. They did not understand his teachings.

Jesus knew their thoughts and wanted to teach them more about his kingdom. We do not know all they talked about that evening. But he taught them many things.

He said, "If you want to be good servants of God, you will obey my words. If you know what I have taught you, you will be happy when you obey them."

Later he said to them, "Love one another." And then he said, "The man who really loves me is the one who does what I have taught."

Jesus told them that he would soon die and leave them alone. But they should not be afraid. "After I rise, I will go ahead of you into Galilee."

Then Jesus and his disciples sang a song and left the upstairs room.

Jesus Dies on a Cross

Matthew 27:1-54; Mark 15:1-39;
Luke 23:1-47; John 18:28—19:30

Jesus had gone all over the country, teaching and helping people. Most of the people were glad to hear him. But a few did not like the things Jesus taught. They found a way to have Jesus arrested. He was brought to the governor, who was a man named Pilate.

Pilate talked with Jesus. Then he said to the crowd, "I find nothing wrong with Jesus." Those who were against Jesus got the crowd to say, "He is a troublemaker

"This man was the son of God"

© 1965 Warner Press, Inc.

all through the country. Crucify him! Crucify him!"

Because Pilate wanted to please the people, he called soldiers and told them to take Jesus away to be crucified.

The soldiers put a crown of thorns upon Jesus' head. They put a purple robe on him, and a stick in his hand. Then they made fun of him. Some of them spit on him, and some hit him. Jesus did not say a word.

At last they took off the purple robe, dressed Jesus in his own clothes, and took him out of the city to be crucified.

Two robbers were to be crucified at the same time. The three carried heavy wooden crosses.

A crowd of people followed. Some were Jesus' friends who wanted to help him and could not. But many in the crowd were not friends of Jesus.

On the hill the soldiers fastened the three men to the crosses. Then they raised the crosses high in the air.

From the cross Jesus prayed, "Father, forgive them, for they do not know what they are doing."

One of the robbers made fun of Jesus. But the other one said, "We have done wrong, but Jesus has not." To Jesus he said, "Lord, remember me when you come into your kingdom."

Jesus answered, "Today you will be with me in Paradise."

The sad friends of Jesus were standing near and saw all that happened. About noon the sky suddenly grew dark. For three hours the great darkness lasted. Then Jesus cried with a loud voice, "It is finished."

A Roman soldier standing by the cross said, "This man was the Son of God."

© 1965 Warner Press

Jesus Rises from the Dead

Matthew 27:57—28:15; Mark 15:45—16:11

After Jesus died on the cross, some of his friends wrapped his body in fine cloth and put the body in a tomb in a garden.

Jesus' enemies had a big stone put at the doorway. And soldiers guarded the tomb.

As it began to get light on Sunday morning, there was an earthquake. The soldiers saw an angel roll away the stone at the door of the tomb. The soldiers were

Jesus had said, "Go at once and tell my friends"

so afraid that they fell to the ground. Later they ran away to the city.

Some women who were friends of Jesus came to the garden. They saw that the stone had been moved. The tomb was empty. They wondered who had taken away Jesus' body.

Then they saw an angel. "Do not be afraid," he said. "Jesus is not here. He has risen as he said. Go quickly and tell his friends that he is alive. He will meet them in Galilee."

How happy the women were! They ran quickly to tell the good news. It seemed almost too wonderful to be true, but they believed it.

Peter and John ran to see the tomb for themselves. They saw that the stone was rolled away from the door. They went inside. But they saw no one. Then they saw the clothes that had been on Jesus' body when it was put into the tomb. Peter and John were sure now that Jesus was alive once more.

On this morning Mary Magdalene stood outside the tomb crying. She saw two angels inside the tomb. They said, "Why are you crying?"

"Because they have taken Jesus away," she answered, "and I do not know where."

Then she turned around, and there stood Jesus. But she did not know him. She thought he was the one who took care of the garden. She said, "Where have you put Jesus?"

Then Jesus said, "Mary!" and she knew his voice. What glad joy was in Mary's heart! She fell at his feet and cried, "Master!"

Jesus said, "Go at once and tell my friends."

Paul Is Shipwrecked
Acts 27

Everywhere Paul went he preached about Jesus. Some of the people who did not believe in Jesus had Paul arrested. Then he had to go to Rome on a ship for a trial.

Sailing was not good, for the winds were strong and blowing from the wrong way. No wonder the people on the ship were glad when they stopped at a little island.

Winter was coming on. Paul told the

Everyone on the ship with Paul reached shore safely

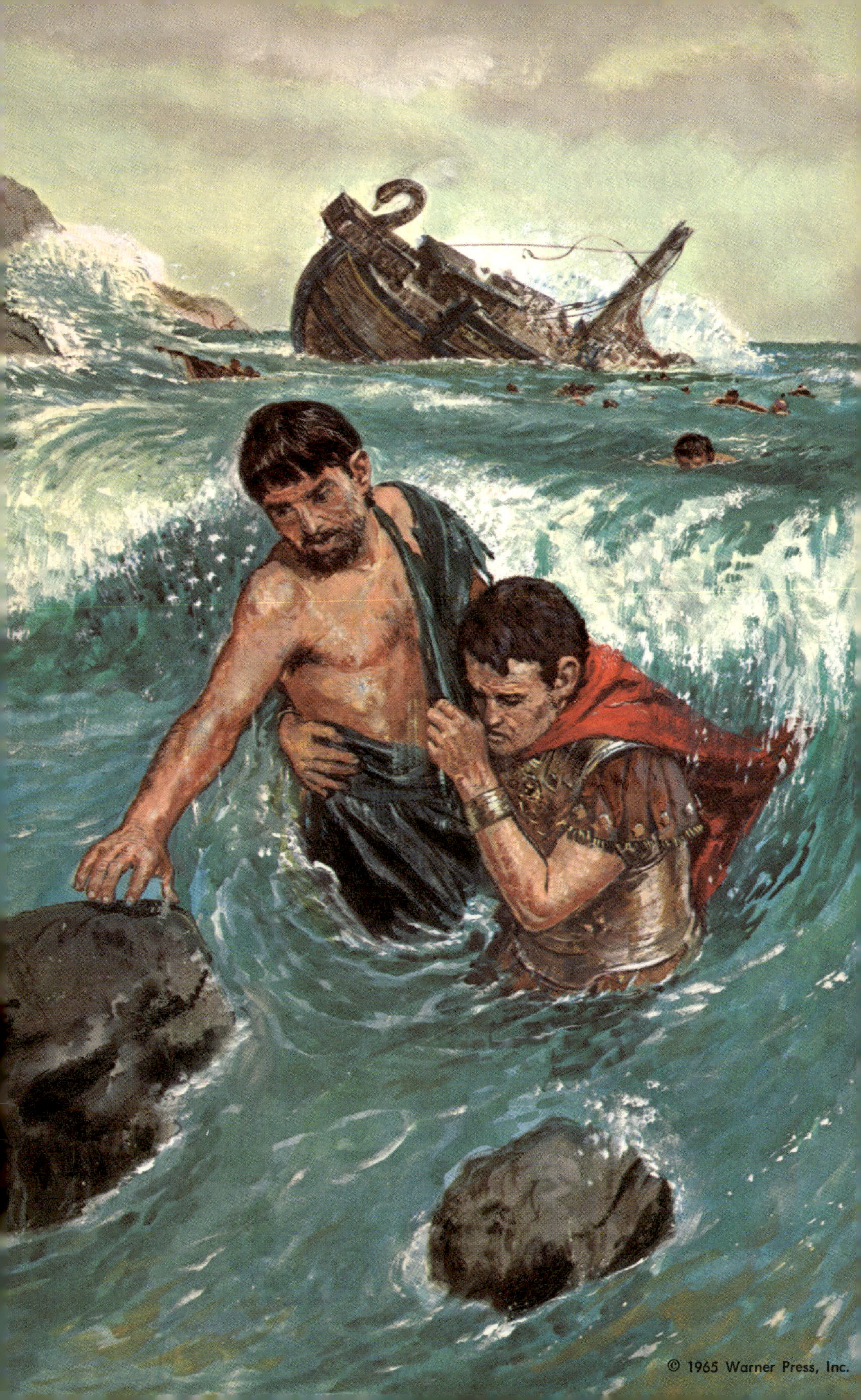

captain, "This will be a dangerous trip if we sail now." But they decided to go to a better place for the winter.

They had not gone far when a great wind came down upon them. How the big waves tossed the ship! They did not know how soon it might be torn in two. Then the captain remembered that Paul had said it was not safe to sail.

They waited for the storm to end, but it went on and on. They could not see the sun by day or the moon by night.

One morning Paul called everyone to him. Above the noise of the storm he said, "Cheer up! Even though we will lose the ship, no one will lose his life. Last night an angel of God told me this."

Still the storm did not stop. Two weeks passed. Then the sailors saw land near. No one knew where they were. They did not know if there were rocks at the shore or sand. They waited for morning to come.

Paul said to them, "You have not eaten for fourteen days. I ask all of you to eat some food. You need it. No one will be lost." Then Paul took some food and gave thanks to God. The people felt better, and they ate some too.

When it was day they could see that there was a sandy shore. But there were big rocks in the water too. They tried to take the ship near the shore, but it got stuck on the rocks. At last the ship began to break up.

All who could swim jumped into the water and swam to shore. The others found parts of the broken ship and floated in to shore. There were two hundred and seventy-six people on the ship, and they all reached shore safely.

The Philippian Jailer

Acts 16:16-34

An angry crowd made its way down the streets, pulling two men along to the prison. There they gave the two men to the jailer.

These men were Paul and Silas, who were Christian missionaries. They had made some people angry because they had helped an unhappy slave girl. Now Paul and Silas were beaten and put in prison.

Paul and Silas were alone in the dark,

The jailer fell on his knees before Paul and Silas

© 1965 Warner Press, Inc.

little room. How their backs hurt! But Paul and Silas were not like the other prisoners. They did not mind that they had been treated badly. They talked to each other about God and his great love. At twelve o'clock they prayed and sang praises to God.

The other prisoners heard the prayers and the songs. Why were these two men so happy? Surely they had been beaten enough to make them sad!

Suddenly a great earthquake shook the prison. The doors came open. The chains that held the prisoners broke.

The jailer woke up and saw that the prison doors were open. He ran to the jail, very much afraid. He knew the rulers would kill him if even one man got away from the prison. Thinking that the prisoners had all run away, he drew his sword to kill himself.

Paul called to him in the dark, "Do not hurt yourself—we are all here."

The jailer called for a light. He hurried into the prison. There he saw all the prisoners. Now he knew that Paul and Silas could not be dangerous men. They must be men of God. He fell at their feet, asking, "Sirs, what must I do to be saved?"

They said, "Believe on the Lord Jesus Christ, and you will be saved." And everyone in the prison heard about Jesus, the Savior of men.

The jailer believed and he was very happy. All the others in his house believed in Jesus too. Before morning Paul and Silas baptized all of them.

© 1965 Warner Press, Inc.

Jon Sep. 10, 1973
20